A YEAR ON THE HILL

WORK BY JIM FISCUS & CHRIS BILHEIMER

GEORGIA MUSEUM OF ART, UNIVERSITY OF GEORGIA

DECEMBER 13, 2014–MARCH 8, 2015

Published by the Georgia Museum of Art, University of Georgia.
All rights reserved. No part of this book may be reproduced
without the written consent of the publishers.

Printed in an edition of 500 by Burman Printing.
Department of Publications: Hillary Brown and Anna Truszczynski
Designer: Chris Bilheimer

Library of Congress Cataloging-in-Publication Data applied for.

Partial support for the exhibitions and programs at the Georgia Museum
of Art is provided by the Georgia Council for the Arts through the
appropriations of the Georgia General Assembly. The Georgia Council
for the Arts also receives support from its partner agency, the National
Endowment for the Arts. Individuals, foundations, and corporations
provide additional support through their gifts to the University of
Georgia Foundation.

This publication was made possible by a generous gift from Todd Emily.

TORN UP NEGS GLUED TO GLASS

MULTI PAGE PAPER NARA - SINGLE IMAGE - CAUSTIC/VARNISH

MULTI IMAGE

CHEMICAL TREATMENT | ACETONE
PAINT/FAUX VIGNETTE | ENCAUSTIC/WAX
                      ACID

PROJECTIONS/CUT NEGS

LIGHTBOX

XEROX

SILICON/TEST

4/c ?

TRANSFER
SANDPAPER ON ACETATE
SCRATCH ACETATE/NEG

MULTIPLE ACETATE LAYERS
LIGHTBOX

DOUBLE PRINT

MULTI IMAGE
SINGLE

TORN
NEG

TRYPTICH
SINGLE
TRANSFER
WIPE

SCRATCH/MULTI
NEG / PAPER

MULTI IMAGE

VIGNETTE - TORN NEG

LIGHT SIGN

SILICONE?
TORN NEG

TRYPTICH

MULTIPAPER

4/c - TORN NEG - LIGHTBOX
              GRID

X BIRDNEST - WHITE
X FROG - STRAIGHT - CUT WHITE / TORN NEG
X GARLIC PLANTS - BW X ON WHITE
X PEARS - 4 PIECE - ON BLACK
X CATFISH - ON WHITE DIP IN INK
XX HANDS - BLACK - SINGLE
  BULL
X PODS/BLACK - WHITE
X CHICKENS - WHITE
X HORSE - WHITE
X MOTHS - WHITE
  CROWS   SCYTHE
X POSSUM BLACK
  KUDZU/CUTTING
  PLANT X BLUE CRAB
  INSECTS/ANTS WHITE
              EGGS

In the essay that follows, Professor Asen Kirin remarks that Jim Fiscus sets out to "erase the once-revered boundaries between commercial and fine-art photography." I would note as well that, in spite of the extreme sophistication of his work, the vernacular snapshot remains in Fiscus's photographic arsenal, although he uses it more to record concepts for an imagined reality than to represent the world faithfully. Professor Kirin notes that Chris Bilheimer is equally determined to dissolve reality into a sort of chaos, a reminder of the randomness present in even the most structured universe, like in the "built" environment of that makeshift barn-studio on the Hill.

Certainly then, this exhibition, so provocative of novel ideas and unexpected aperçus, is a testament to these two artists' vision as well as to their collaborative process. We are pleased to present the exhibition once again to our publics, both academic and lay, here in Athens, where, in 2011, Fiscus and Bilheimer first showed this work at the University of Georgia's Lamar Dodd School of Art. We are grateful that they allow us the privilege of sharing their vision with generations of students now and in the future. We offer profound thanks as well to Dr. Kirin; through his words, he allows us to join in his perception of a universe where two gifted and thoughtful artists recompose nature.

—William Underwood Eiland
Director, Georgia Museum of Art

PROCESS TESTS:

- XACTO SCRATCH NEGS
- SAND PAPER ON ACETATE/BACKLIT
- CYMK B/W SILVER PRINTS W/BLEACH
- GLUE 2 CHROMES TOGETHER
- ACETONE VIGNETTE
- ENCAUSTIC/BEESWAX
- WOOD VARNISH ON XEROX
- MUROTIC ACID ON ACETATE PRINT
- EVEN LAYER OF SILICONE
- ACID ON FLOURECENT LIGHT HOUSING
- ACETONE WIPE OF NEGATIVE (COMPLETT)
- DOUBLE PRINT AFTER ACETONE WIPE

BIRDSNEST

SHOOT ON WHITE

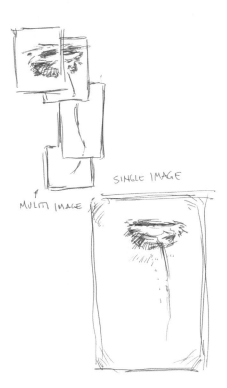

MULTI IMAGE

SINGLE IMAGE

Nearly twenty years ago, photographer and native Texan Jim Fiscus chose to make a home for his family in the state of Georgia, even though his business as a commercial photographer required prolonged stays in New York City, Los Angeles, and London. During the winter of 2008, after a profound change in his personal life, the artist moved to a small rock cottage in the woods covering a rise known as "the Hill" in the outskirts of Athens, Georgia. Between the end of 2009 and the fall of 2010, he collaborated with designer Chris Bilheimer on a series of large-scale, close-up photographic prints of plants and animals.

Bilheimer made Athens his home for more than twenty years after he left Los Angeles. In Georgia, he began a self-guided course of study as a photographer and graphic designer, utilizing novel techniques to achieve unique visual effects, which led to his position as art director for R.E.M. His experience with client work, predominantly with musicians, led to him viewing his work as not solely his own, but a product of a collaborative process in which he did not have complete control. His portfolio consists of screenshots of David Letterman holding up albums he has designed, and his work has defined the visual presence of bands from R.E.M. to Green Day.

Fiscus may not be a household name, but hundreds of millions of people across the world have seen his commissioned photographs. His distinctive images are rendered in what has been called the "Fiscus look," one of viscous radiance and abundant, crisp detail, known to both corporate clients and connoisseurs of photography. Notably, he has worked with television networks and channels, including HBO, A&E, and Channel Four London. In the United States, advertisements for shows on the premium cable network Showtime, including *Dexter, Brotherhood, Shameless*, and most recently *Homeland,* are his best-known work. For each of these shows, Fiscus created portfolios of photographs that were at once severe and lighthearted, blending visual jests and historical iconography. By contemplating recent and current television series through an art-historical prism, the photographer created a visual cultural commentary on these notable examples of contemporary storytelling. Like other prominent present-day image-makers, he sets out to erase the boundaries between commercial and fine-art photography.

Fiscus's work has a blend of wholesomeness and darkness, so it is hardly a surprise that the photographer was always drawn to the art of both Norman Rockwell and Joel-Peter Witkin. In a visit to Athens in 2008, Witkin, a man of few words and fewer compliments, told Fiscus that the quality of light in his work was exceptional when looking at his prints. As far back as 1992, when he first experimented with digital manipulations in his photographs, Fiscus redid Norman Rockwell's *Saying Grace* (1951). The re-creation of this painting involved the fusion of separate photographs each featuring one object or figure in the original composition. The result is a pictorial space that has the veracity of a snapshot and yet defies common sense because a camera could never capture the composition as rendered. Thus, the convincing but impossible space of Fiscus's diner spins together several art-historical threads—the illusion of spatial depth (linear perspective) and the Old Masters of Western painting, Rockwell's humble illustrations, and photography's ability to document physical reality. Fiscus wants the viewer to think about both this specific pictorial place and the act of looking at images as the products of cultural construction.

Like Fiscus, Bilheimer was drawn to the way in which Rockwell depicted life but with an interest in exposing an undercurrent of darkness. Both have searched for, as Bilheimer puts it, "the cracks in the veneer," seeking to capture the good and bad without judgment and discovering, or perhaps creating, the very shadows that seem to underlie wholesome depictions of reality. Bilheimer found that his own obsession with detail stifled rather than enhanced his work. Frustrated, he sought ways of artistic expression that rendered control unnecessary. As he says, "In my world, nothing ever turned out the way you planned, so I learned to stop planning and just start creating and see where it went."

***

The images in the Hill series consider the power of photography to impose meaning on humans' material surroundings. There is an autobiographical layer to these photographs that illustrate the struggle to restore a sense of wholeness to a shattered life (*Nest, Crows, Raccoon, Grasshopper,* and *Moth*). Fiscus shows us how he did just that while secluded in his rock cottage. In his hermitage, he lived in the moment and let himself be fully absorbed by the ethos of the Hill—this leafy model of the world where the past is invented and literally reassembled. In this manner, he faced loss, aestheticized death (*Frog* and *Lizard*), and glorified the humblest of plants (*Sumac, Thistle,* and *T-Plant*).

Lee Epting, a local luminary, businessman, and conservationist, created what he calls "an orphanage for old homes" on the Hill, which became Fiscus's home and studio. Epting moved and reassembled historic houses from Georgia and across the Southeast, selecting the perfect spot for these architectural transplants, which look as if they have always been there. Although elevated, the Hill does not command sweeping vistas. Instead, its screening woods wrap around every clearing so that the gaze of a dweller or visitor is always directed inwards.

Fiscus, Bilheimer, and the photography team set up a makeshift studio in Epting's dark, old barn, which holds various salvaged architectural fragments (pages 44, 46). In the center rose the spotlights, large-view analog camera, and stand with elaborate backdrop paintings by Bilheimer. The natural light streaming in through the cracks between the wood planks of this dark chamber molded columns, cornices, and mantels and filtered through old glass panels of windows and doors leaning against the walls. The sense of wonder the environment created was enhanced by the energy of the project and made fresh by the involvement of Fiscus's young son, Ellis, who pushed the shutter release on many photographs as his father held him. In this space, the artists and their team created a work of performance art that toyed with the phenomenon of the darkroom, which channels outside light in order to superimpose an image on a two-dimensional surface. In the most unassuming way, the set reenacted the invention of photography, calling to mind the *camera obscura* and *camera lucida*.

The bustling action in and around the barn was preceded by months of planning and scores of preparatory drawings of different subjects, compositions, visual qualities, and technical considerations by Fiscus and Bilheimer (pages 4, 6). Fiscus browsed albums with reproductions of plant and animal drawings from the *Vienna Dioscurides* vellum folio from 515 CE (commissioned by the Roman imperial princess Anicia Juliana) to Albrecht Dürer's watercolor *Great Piece of Turf* (1503; Albertina, Vienna) and Leonardo da Vinci's drawing *Ornithogalum* (*Star of Bethlehem*) (ca. 1500; Royal Collection of Queen Elizabeth II). Additional excitement came from the exhibition catalogue *The Flowering of Florence: Botanical Art for the Medici* (2002, National Gallery of Art, Washington, D.C.).

Bilheimer served as a foil to Fiscus's planned, thorough process, bringing to this collaboration his strategy of "introducing chaos or random aberrations to achieve an expression untouched by the obsession with control," which led the project to develop a life of its own. Bilheimer described the process: "We would scrap ideas halfway through. While on the way to shoot something we had planned for weeks, we would grab a plant from the side of the road and shoot it instead. After days of creating experimental backdrops in the studio, I would paint new backdrops on the spot. Jim handled all of the principal photography, but once it was shot, I would often take over, tearing up pieces and trying to glue them back or pouring acid on the negatives to see what happened." According to Bilheimer, *Grasshopper* sums up the entire collaborative experience. Fiscus carefully photographed the dead insect, documenting it with countless large-format Polaroid negatives until he captured the perfect image. During transport between the barn and the house, a small object fell into the water bath with the negatives. Each movement of the water bath led the object to scratch the previously pristine negative, creating an unintentional set of flaws. The crisp detail of the image combined with the randomness of the scratches captures the divergent processes of both artists.

In the end, the portfolio of images serves as a reflection on the millennia-old tradition of botanical and zoological illustration in Western art. The artists deliberately draw parallels between the close-up-and-blow-up approach and the practices of the Accademia dei Lincei (Academy of the Lynx-Eyed), established in early seventeenth-century Florence when Galileo's telescope turned away from celestial bodies to focus on botanical, zoological, and mineral specimens. This inward gaze started a new era in the scientific exploration of the material world, with artists who belonged to the academy executing a series of now famous drawings from nature (many of them housed in Buckingham Palace). In its take on this tradition, this photographic series sets the stage for an experience that commences as a contemplation of nature promising to yield self-knowledge, then delves into the intertwined history of natural science and the visual arts. The "Fiscus look" guides our experience of the material world through the prism of a deific hyperrealism, suggestive of an altarpiece from the Renaissance. These colossal photographs rendering small, lowly parts of our organic surroundings embody the new humanism in which man does not dominate nature but instead partakes in the existence of the animate and the inanimate.

—Asen Kirin

Dr. Asen Kirin is an associate professor of art and the associate director of the University of Georgia's Lamar Dodd School of Art. Kirin studied the history of art and architecture during his graduate studies in the United States. He holds an MA from Vanderbilt University and a PhD from Princeton.

JIM FISCUS AND CHRIS BILHEIMER

LEE'S HANDS, 2010
PHOTOCOPY
DIPTYCH, 122 x 36 INCHES EACH

DESTROYED AFTER EXHIBITION

A YEAR ON THE HILL

WORK BY JIM FISCUS & CHRIS BILHEIMER

JIM FISCUS AND CHRIS BILHEIMER

CATFISH, 2010
DIGITAL PRINT
96 x 56 INCHES

Georgia Museum of Art, University of Georgia; Gift of the artists

JIM FISCUS AND CHRIS BILHEIMER

CROWS, 2010
DIGITAL PRINT
TRIPTYCH, 42 x 36 INCHES EACH

PRIVATE COLLECTION

JIM FISCUS AND CHRIS BILHEIMER

LIZARD, 2010
DIGITAL PRINT
81 x 58 INCHES

GEORGIA MUSEUM OF ART, UNIVERSITY OF GEORGIA; GIFT OF THE ARTISTS

JIM FISCUS AND CHRIS BILHEIMER

MOTH, 2010
DIGITAL PRINT
45 1/2 x 44 INCHES

GEORGIA MUSEUM OF ART, UNIVERSITY OF GEORGIA; GIFT OF THE ARTISTS

JIM FISCUS AND CHRIS BILHEIMER

GRASSHOPPER, 2010
DIGITAL PRINT
58 x 70 INCHES

GEORGIA MUSEUM OF ART, UNIVERSITY OF GEORGIA; GIFT OF THE ARTISTS

JIM FISCUS AND CHRIS BILHEIMER

FROG, 2010
DIGITAL PRINT
82 x 58 INCHES

GEORGIA MUSEUM OF ART, UNIVERSITY OF GEORGIA; GIFT OF THE ARTISTS

JIM FISCUS AND CHRIS BILHEIMER

SUMAC, 2010
DIGITAL PRINTS AND ACRYLIC
TRIPTYCH, 56 x 28 INCHES EACH

GEORGIA MUSEUM OF ART, UNIVERSITY OF GEORGIA; GIFT OF THE ARTISTS

JIM FISCUS AND CHRIS BILHEIMER

THISTLE, 2010
DIGITAL PRINT
48 x 24 INCHES

GEORGIA MUSEUM OF ART, UNIVERSITY OF GEORGIA; GIFT OF THE ARTISTS

JIM FISCUS AND CHRIS BILHEIMER

RACCOON, 2010
DIGITAL PRINT
75 x 58 INCHES

PRIVATE COLLECTION

JIM FISCUS AND CHRIS BILHEIMER

CHICKEN, 2010
DIGITAL PRINT
TRIPTYCH, 48 X 48 INCHES EACH

PRIVATE COLLECTION

JIM FISCUS AND CHRIS BILHEIMER

CHICKEN, 2010
DIGITAL PRINT
TRIPTYCH, 48 x 48 INCHES EACH

PRIVATE COLLECTION

JIM FISCUS AND CHRIS BILHEIMER

CHICKEN, 2010
DIGITAL PRINT
TRIPTYCH, 48 x 48 INCHES EACH

PRIVATE COLLECTION

JIM FISCUS AND CHRIS BILHEIMER

NEST, 2010
DIGITAL PRINT AND ACRYLIC
72 x 58 INCHES

JIM FISCUS

A native Texan, Jim Fiscus got his first taste of photography at a bullfight in Mexico when he was six years old. His dad gave him a camera, and his uncle goaded him to use up the entire roll of film, which he promptly did. He studied briefly at East Texas State University under his mentor, Jim Newberry, and, in the years since, has become known for his cinematic style and ability to tell a story in a single frame. His work can be seen in campaigns for clients ranging from Showtime, HBO, A&E, and Britain's ITV to Levi's, Credit Suisse, and Motorola. Fiscus makes his home in Athens, Georgia, with his wife and two kids in a house built in 1826.

CHRIS BILHEIMER

Born in 1970 in Los Angeles, California, Chris Bilheimer moved to Athens, Georgia, to study drawing and painting at the Lamar Dodd School of Art at the University of Georgia. Sidelined by his interest in the local music scene, he began a self-taught study of graphic design and photography outside of the university system. He accepted a job as art director for R.E.M. before finishing his degree and has continued to work for the band for the last twenty years. Bilheimer has worked as a freelance designer for the music industry, most notably for the bands Green Day and Widespread Panic, and recently he branched out into the film industry, designing movie posters for feature films and documentaries. After twenty-two years in Athens, he and his wife recently relocated to Austin, Texas.

ACKNOWLEDGMENTS

Jim and Chris would like to thank the following people for
their support and hard work in helping us create this show.

HILLARY BILHEIMER

LEE EPTING

ELLIS JAMES FISCUS

ANDREA FREMIOTTI

EMILY HALL

MARK OWERKO

ANDREA SMITH

BOOK DESIGN: CHRIS BILHEIMER
DOCUMENTARY PHOTOGRAPHY: EMILY HALL & JIM FISCUS